MW01105087

City
THAT
Ripens
ON THE
Tree
OF THE
World

Poems by Robin Davidson

CALYPSO EDITIONS

CALYPSO EDITIONS
www.CalypsoEditions.org

By unearthing literary gems from previous generations, translating
foreign writers into English with integrity, and providing a space for
talented new voices, Calypso Editions is committed to publishing
books that will endure in both content and form.
Our only criterion is excellence.

Cover photo: *Orchids and Lace (Kraków Balcony)*
by Ewa Elżbieta Nowakowska
Author photo by Tony Davidson

Book Layout & Cover Design: Anthony Bonds
www.goldenratiodesign.anthonybonds.com

ISBN 10: 0-9887903-0-0
ISBN 13: 978-0-9887903-0-8

First edition, July 2013
Printed in the United States

This book has been funded in part by the Houston Arts Alliance
Individual Artist Grant Program (2009).

for Ewa Lipska and for Kraków

"The cities that ripen on the tree of the world are enclosed in shape like apples . . . . The city trodden by feet and the city in which thoughts swirl adjoin each other at the lens of the eye, by which they are scrupulously separated. Even the blind see what is most important: limitless darkness like the night sky, in which the constellations of the names of all things are scattered, shining and dying like stars."

—*Dreams and Stones* by Magdalena Tulli
(Translated by Bill Johnston)

Contents

7   Mrs. Schmetterling Kneels in a Garden

8   An Ascension

10   City that Ripens on the Tree of the World

12   Window

13   Dusk in Jordan Park

14   Loom

15   Św. Maria Magdalena Pisząca

16   Sorites and Sand

17   Self-Portrait: Trieste

18   The Palace at 4:00 a.m.

20   The Angel of Architecture

21   Mrs. Schmetterling Thinks of Her Heart

22   The Rothko Chapel, Houston, Early Spring

25   Mrs. Schmetterling Considers the Beautiful

26   Portrait of the Artist's Wife with Pegasus

27   In an Amsterdam Hotel

28   Notes for a Larger Poem

29   Revisions

32   Viaticum

33   August Garden

35   In the Balance of Final Things

36   Oświęcim

38   Borowski's Suicide

39   In Kazimierz

40   Winter Litany

41   How to Paint Light

42   What Mrs. Schmetterling Wants

44   Notes

47   Acknowledgments

City

THAT

Ripens

ON THE

Tree

OF THE

World

MRS. SCHMETTERLING KNEELS IN A GARDEN

for Ewa Lipska

Mrs. Schmetterling, let's call her Judith, married.
She is neither great musician nor poet.
Not scientist nor historian. She is ordinary.
Any century's woman. She cooks, reads, bathes children
and dogs. She takes out the garbage, listens to music.
Mrs. Schmetterling is tired. Her imagination is
pressed like a tiny chestnut blossom between the pages
of old letters and recipes, a book of days.
She would like to give herself advice, chide herself not
to remain invisible, feeding on the erotic bread
of great art. But she doesn't. She hesitates, keeps herself
at arm's length. A practice she learned from her mother.
Instead she kneels in a garden, breaks open
each amaryllis pod in her palm, peels back
the green triangles of skin forming the bolus
left from the blossom and sprinkles
the black ash of seedlings onto the clay.

An Ascension

after a photograph by Daria Tuminas, St. Petersburg

I.

What we see first are the feet, a woman suspended
in midair from the unseen—whether rafter or rope
or branch of an invisible tree—
then the toenails polished green as leaves
in the hem of her floral dress.
The gazer's eye moves on, among coat and chair,
shawl and blanket, the open cigarette pack,
matches, ashtray, the last palpable newsprint
she will hold in her invisible hands. All of this
rests on the floor's rough-hewn wood—
like an ancient tree flayed and stretched beneath her.
And so we assume the worst:
A woman steps from the chair's edge to hang herself
like a dress in the room's close dark.

II.

In the middle of his own life's path, Dante
began to write his way out of exile.
He needed saving from his own rage. An inferno
turned ascension he would name
poetry, then love, then mystical sainthood.
He invented the *Wood of the Suicides* as reminder:
Those who take their own lives lose the right
to live again in human form. Dante believed

he must follow the call of the Rood,
not the shrill cry of snapped branches,
the tormented soul speaking. He must leave
the domain of poets in order to ascend.
No empathy among the angels.

III.

In the essay Yeats called "Magic," Eden
is a walled garden on a mountain summit two miles
high. And from the garden's center the Tree
of Knowledge rises. In its branches the birds build
their nests, and angels stand among them.
And this same tree is the Tree of Life
where sighing souls move in its branches
instead of sap, whose apples bear human faces,
and if you placed your ear close enough,
you could hear within the tree's fruit
the struggle of voices trapped in an inner dark.

IV.

Dante and Yeats believed in other worlds, in the tree
as emissary for creation's complex paradox—
but the woman here, whose feet reveal her,
believes only in the reach for light,
follows the call of the simple tree
growing in her mind. First, green figs
then a weightlessness and a rising.
Her entire body afloat in the night sky, ascending.

CITY THAT RIPENS ON THE TREE OF THE WORLD

The tree outside Mrs. Schmetterling's flat
is a cathedral. Its black branches are stones

luminous with ice windows.
The tree's single chorister's a black and white magpie

whose visible grace is a persistent scavenging.
She knows such scavenging.

She loves this bird.
Mrs. Schmetterling watches the November

seasonal seam open to a dual harvest.
She lives at an intersection

where Krupnicza Street crosses Mickiewicz Avenue,
where barley and the great Romantic poet collide.

When night falls, Mrs. Schmetterling will see
two moons rise outside her window,

like laundry hung out piece by piece
over a balcony in winter wind. One pure, bright,

the original moon. The other, its shadow
or some odd reflection caught

on the outside of the glass in the branches. No,
they hang in the inner lace of curtains along her desk,

so that she stands, takes the lace in her hands,
turns it to the left, the right.

But this doubleness stays.
Twin sisters of half-light, side by side

hovering above her. If only one of them turned,
the moon would be full.

WINDOW

It is my first afternoon in Kraków. At the back of the Franciscan Church,
I see the Wyspiański window where God creates the world
with a single stroke. Hair, body swirling, fluid
like the robes of a wizard, he is a flying mane, a glass hand—
upraised, poised for touch but suspended there, throbbing—
the October Polish sun for a moment flooding the room.

In the photograph it is 1978. My father stands in the kitchen
of my grandmother's old house on Ruby Drive.
In his left hand he holds a glass of scotch. His right is raised above his head,
fingers outstretched as if to wave to the camera, or bless the others.
He is drunk with the presence of all he loves
gathered in a single room.

This is when I first know our world is a window:
Porous realm of what is or was or could be.

Dusk in Jordan Park, *ul. Ingardena, Kraków*
for Adam Zagajewski

The shoulders of the poets are covered with snow.
Their eye sockets are lined with ice.
Even the composer is silent, each circle and staff of
his mind's music, frozen flat in a field of white.

I move my ungloved hand along these old half-figures,
    trace each name twice—
        Mickiewicz, Słowacki, Chopin, Kochanowski—

Stone ghosts, I ask you,
are you human treasure wrenched from ruin and kept?
Are you home in the clay which holds you?
Or do you long to walk, as I do,
ordinary among the living

slang of streets, deformed noses of the old drunks,
the hollyhocks and mud lathering the hollow of old lap
of the *pani* whose skirts brush my ankles
when she asks me my first name?

I continue my circular walk, watch the slow snow
fall like stars forming behind the eyes
as if a chronic migraine had begun, as relentless as history's pulse
until all paths of this labyrinthine garden,

        pruned shrubs, wooden benches, towering pines,
      are powdered with a rose-white-light-going-blue.

LOOM

It was not a question of deceit but of survival
that she sat long nights in moonlight at the loom,
and what she wove by day in verdant colors, by night
with blue-streaked eyes, she would unravel,
stitching in the half-illumined dark
another fabric, each shuttle's stroke, a stirring
like a wingbeat in the surface of
a shawl almost translucent, a second skin.

All she knew moved through her skin
until, tongueless, she sang the colors of fire,
her threads, the words of a room
among rooms in the larger dwelling,
until out of the golden fabric of her shroud,
a woman rose up.

ŚW. MARIA MAGDALENA PISZĄCA

Saint Mary Magdalene Writing
by the Master of the Female Half-Figures (Antwerp)
Czartoryski Museum, Kraków

In the first half of the sixteenth century the painter resurrects her,
dresses her not as the Jewess mourning her dead lover
but as Christian noblewoman, the Renaissance crimson of her bust line
half-hidden in black velvet sleeves which open first onto forearms—
cuffed in lace, each layer banded by ribbon, its gilt embroidery—
and then onto wrists, elongated fingers, the poised quill.

　　She is in the mind of the man who makes her a woman forgiven
of poverty, passion, her first profession.
Her head is covered, bowed to the page,
fifteen hundred years of letters or poems or prayers
accumulating in her hands.

She is alone, composed and composing. No god's voice
asks—*woman, why are you weeping?*—her reverie, a painted peace
assumed by a man whose hands believe in sainthood.
He has given her comforts—coffee urn, ink well, the desk's smooth surface.
As proof of lyric time or of eternity, he has hung
a clock behind her—its red face reads 8:40, morning, a winter sun.

　　This writing is her first task, whether joy or torment,
and she opens all of her body to it so that morning light
moves through her as if she were window grating or gauze or porous soul.
She must be cold, so much of her shoulders exposed.
She must be tired, sitting so long.

Sorites and Sand

Mrs. Schmetterling has been thinking about boundaries,
how the borders of countries and of gardens overlap,
how words themselves melt into one another—prefix, suffix, root—
until she is now swept away
in a sea of sentence upon sentence, drowning.
Recently she learned she has confused the words
sostre and *sorites*, *sisters* and *a heap of sand*.
What words she wonders are necessary for sister
syllogisms to build upon each other,
not by heaping but weaving,
like the loom work of a great queen.
Mrs. Schmetterling could build a kingdom
on the threads of a shroud. She could stretch strands
of cowhide wide to build a city.
She could be a woman poised to speak
if these thoughts running wild in her head
could converge, compose the seamless fabric
of a slow-moving river, each syllable,
a rivulet, a warp or weft thread
floated inextricably into each sister stitch,
world to word, word to world.

SELF-PORTRAIT: TRIESTE

I am listening for what is not there,
the tonality of silence, the blank space
between the spoken lines of a conversation,
what lives in the eyes, the lilt of a head.
I know nothing more
of history, American soldiers, than the smell
of one man's green uniform,
the cold metallic stars on his chest.
I accumulate the absences, study them,
as if they were the rhinestone buttons
on my mother's best suit, shining like stars,
but not stars. I will learn to live
by the boundaries language makes,
a child tottering at the edge
of speech and an old mattress
in a Trieste hotel room at the border
of Italy, Yugoslavia, Slovenia—
forty, fifty years of naming, renaming.

THE PALACE AT 4:00 A.M.

Memory's nakedness is like a bone that will not decay.
–Liu Xiaobo

Alberto Giacometti understood the house of childhood
to be a house of bones, or more accurately

in this case, of bare wood, glass, wire—
the sculpture's naked frame, a skeleton of mother memory.

What I remember as a child is a dream in which I walk
along the steel girders of an anonymous building,

a labyrinth of metal rising into the night sky's
pitch black, the narrow beams like blocks of ice or fire

beneath my feet, each step a tightrope dance above an abyss.
Unlike the *Palace* no objects hang seductively.

No Surrealist's invitation into sleep. I wander endlessly
from beam to beam, imprisoned in an emptiness

whose only gift is silence.
Mother was an absence. The invisible

walls of a house. An empty amphitheater strung with
rhinestones shining like stars.

Mother. An elusive sparkling.
Giacometti divides the *Palace* with a pane of glass,

a transparent skin, a membrane, what we see but cannot touch,
what cannot touch us, a brittle veil between lives.

If I could speak to the girl suspended, balancing,
holding her breath, I would tell her how she will outlive

the inner dark, how the glass pane will shatter
into cerulean fragments, how she will come to wear

these shards like buttons sewn on a woman's suit coat.
Each tiny stone, a star or bone, fastened against her chest

by frayed thread whispering *open, open*,
to each rib, vertebra, as a voice in a dream might

choreograph the tenuous constellation of hours,
burning coals, lemon balm, a flowering.

THE ANGEL OF ARCHITECTURE

You are the one I call in my sleep,
mother of absences, the one whose doorways
grow wide, open onto side yards, gardens
where ferns and the thorny vines of bougainvillea
trail among rocks and the terra cotta tiles.
Your body is a trellis for climbing
jasmine and the orphaned world.
You wear stucco and smooth-cut stone.
Your moss-stained dress offers walls
to those whose beds sit among ashes,
under bridges, float on slow-moving rivers.
You appear on downtown streets
in the largest of cities, in dung heaps,
old appliance stores, abandoned warehouses.
You hover above the fire sale, the hands
of women peddling losses, and weave
with fingers which stream like hair,
like rivulets of iron-sweet milk
from your breasts, the house of childhood,
the heart's medieval architecture.

MRS. SCHMETTERLING THINKS OF HER HEART

Mrs. Schmetterling thinks of herself as a visible whole
not as parts, a conglomeration of molecules.
She is not a scientific woman.
When she thinks of heart, that rocking, flopping in her chest,
she does not see in her mind's eye a muscle
or chambers, or bloody arteries twitching, rather
she sees cranes rising from a marsh *en masse*,
their extended wings a white blanket of fluttering
that propel her to her feet and then to the mailbox.
She loves letters, or the thought of letters,
and the oceans they have crossed, braiding the world
together like a handful of hair resting along her shoulder.
She is enviable in this way, for she makes all things
rise up from within. Even the most disparate of objects or ideas—
the reading of Wittgenstein's *Tractatus* and schnitzel recipes,
the map pencil drawings of her childhood
and the hubris of war's vowels, Lwów, Lvov, L'viv—
seem to coalesce within her own warm body,
her own inner life and the world's.

THE ROTHKO CHAPEL, HOUSTON, EARLY SPRING

I sit in a room of black paintings, listening to the walls of day open into darkness,
when a shaft of light at the ceiling's center moves into one canvas, creates an opening
purple, rose, and what I hear instead of silence is a line, a poet's voice,

> *God sent me to the sea for pearls.*

If I could, I would follow the call glowing in the painting's lower corner,
enter the gray-black surface and sail the turbulence which is every hero's sea.

A boy I loved believed he could enter a rock with his thumbnail. He would trace
the invisible crack in the stone's surface his grandfather had polished
that he might sail the darkness, find whatever he could in a rock formed by fire.

I sit in a room of black paintings, chapel walls silent as stones, and as inanimate, until

> *God sent me to the sea for pearls*

becomes the storyline breaking out of time at the water's edge,
looking from the porch of the sea onto the sea's dark expanse, and diving
into that rhythmic infinite for the stone one must pull from the clay bottom, gray matter,
the luminous rock within the stone of the oyster, the skull.
The sea-stone is a pearl.

But I meant to sing about the boy I loved who dreamed in his madness he had
swallowed a pearl—
a god making the stories of men, a man making the stories of gods,
a boy building song out of story. I sit in a room of paintings no longer black, listening,
and what I hear instead of silence is a line, a voice, the boy speaking:

> *Every dream is ancient: A boy lives by the River Min*
> *in the province of Sichuan, gathers grasses for his living,*
> *and when one day he pulls from the soil a pearl tinged with rose,*
> *he buries it in his mother's rice jar.*

Grass, rice, coins in abundance make a village covetous,
and when they come to seize the boy's treasure, he swallows the jewel,
his belly burns with thirst until he drinks the river dry,
and his back swells with scales and wings,
the sky with rain, a mother's heart with tears.

This is the story of the dragon's pearl, of a culture's call for creation
and what belongs to a people belongs to the one man. The myth of a pearl becomes
the story of a boy who wanted to die, to let the river enter him until he was cold as stone,
until the stone of madness he imagined lodged in his skull could shine,

illuminate a world.
These are the paintings of a man who wanted to die, to penetrate stone until he
        could not see,
a blind man wanting a second chance, second sight.

                    God sent them to the sea for pearls.

These are the paintings of a man who wanted to live,
to return from stone in a burst of light, rose-tinged, a pearl, a coin, a luminous other.

This is the struggle between story and song.
The pearl is the rock animated, the clay bottom resurrected and ascending.

                    God sends us to the sea for pearls,

for luminous stone, animated by the call of creation.

The boy I loved wanted to die listening to the sea. He believed, in death, he could
        penetrate stone,
enter the rock-hard earth with his thumbnail, rose-colored half-mooned cuticle of stone
digging into darkness, into the blood-black river of his wrist.

The boy I loved wanted to live, a pearl, a coin, a luminous other life he would invent, ancient life, beckoned by an ancient call. He believed he must die to begin again.

I sit in a room of paintings purple and black and rose, listening to light, the voices of the dead swelling like a sea in the back of my skull, and I look at my hands, ask them for a spell, a god's incantatory call to dust.

In memory of Ian Davidson
(1962–2012)

Mrs. Schmetterling Considers the Beautiful

Mrs. Schmetterling looks on beauty
as an interior landscape, the moonrise of her imagination.
When she closes her eyes, she sees the room's ceiling
fill first with billowing shadows, then a pinpoint of
light that blooms into a blue-black shining, then
the brilliant blue of coronal plasma that could
be the widening eye of God. Or a host of
angels navigating a great abyss, their
wings clapping out light. But Mrs. Schmetterling is
skeptical of the sublime. She does not trust a transcendence
that will come to her on the day the world ends.
She believes in what she can see, hold
in her mind's eye. Cold, hard snow
in muddy clumps melting, kicked aside.
Chestnut trees lining the avenues, their tiny candelabras
of blossom upon blossom, at the bud's edge, waiting.
Ubiquitous sparrows flitting among the branches,
then among tulips when they bloom at last.
The romantic vestige of old musicians
spilling their song into the square.
The other music of boot clicks
on stone. All this she carries
as the roiling blue that rises
like a wall, a tidal wave
of light behind her eyes.

Portrait of the Artist's Wife with Pegasus

Józef Mehoffer, oil on canvas, 1914

Behind her, the whole of Art Nouveau frolics—
a white and red beribboned Pegasus
prances in a night sky,
bare-breasted mermaids stream hair
and scaled tails,
bob in a William Morris wallpaper sea
and swoon skyward
into the chest of the horse—

while she sits dressed in black
from the wide-brimmed ruffled hat, feather boa,
to the leather gloves laid flat
on the chintz skirt
smoothed carefully over her knees.
Even her wrists are covered,
one inch of ornamental lace fanning
out from the sleeve.

All of this the artist observes with precision,
but what she sees
is her husband's face
tethered to the canvas as if by invisible thread,
and she has dressed in black
because she mourns
the direction of the light
in his eyes.

In an Amsterdam Hotel

In an Amsterdam hotel we push twin beds together
so that I can lie lengthwise against your back.

We have been here five days, and each morning
I wake to a black and white photograph,

the kind you see in any decent hotel room
where buildings, trees, shrubs stand at a shoreline,

and are mirrored in the water below.
Twin landscapes each growing out of the other,

an irony of rootedness that rises, falls,
then manages this meeting at margin of lake and sky.

It is an ordinary scene, typical I think,
of the photographer's fascination with doubleness,

a halving of the world into positive and negative,
what we are, defined by what we are not,

what we love, by what we must let go.
On these mattresses, our bodies are a landscape of rootedness.

In only a few hours we will rise, dress,
meet separate planes headed for separate continents,

and test the hypothesis of landscape photographers
on separate shorelines.

Notes for a Larger Poem

I am on a train or in a room moving
    slowly, rhythmically into sunrise.
        The windows, jewel-like,

refract the landscape into fragments
    barely visible, blurred, vanishing.
        I turn away.

In the room's corner is a cardboard box
    holding all that is left
        of my father.

Shreds of his best suit and a green blanket.
    The smell of starch, tweed, old shaving lotion,
        the body of memory, rotting . . .

I kneel, cradle the box like a child
    or would, if my arms could reach,
        but the enormity of space

opening before me becomes a blankness
    so large, I cannot yet imagine it
        a possibility for more

than dissolution.

Revisions

A man searches for God.
He searches the dark cavities of libraries,
drinks each book like water out of rock,
ingests the thin white pages,
a manna he holds in his mouth until it sings.
He searches fire escapes, paintings, subways.
He searches restaurants, Roman temples,
his own ruins. When he dreams,
he seeks a heavenly father
to replace the earthly one, long vanished,
and when he wakes, he searches the still sacred
body of his wife for a god, for a father,
for a son. When a son comes,
he glimpses the beginning of divinity,
calls him angel, and tells the boy a story
of the milk-white steed made of lightning
an angel harnessed
to carry a great prophet to heaven.

A man searches for God.
He searches biblical texts, histories, the ambitions
of philosophers. He walks on his hands,
turns the world upside down. He runs and runs.
He searches the constant humming in his head,
searches his Welsh father's poems
for the tune he carries in his chest,
within the sea-green sky of a coat
where metallic stars float, form tiny constellations.
He seeks a heavenly father
to replace the earthly one, long dead,

searches the sacred body of his wife for a god,
for a father, for a son, but no son comes.
The man has a daughter, a Thumbelina of divinity.
Each day he reads to her, she listens
until all the gods of the world
live in her eyes, and there he sees
his own small reflection.

A woman searches for God.
She searches temples and books, altar cloths and gardens.
She searches the center of peonies,
the face of each man she has loved.
She searches her husband's chest, each shoulder,
the smooth, dark skin beneath his eyes.
The woman has a son and in this child's face
she glimpses the beginning of divinity:
God in diapers, God in a baseball cap,
God with a Fender Stratocaster strapped to his chest.
What he creates with his breath, his hands
is reenactment, a legacy of absence.
His song is the grief of a woman who is no son,
the grief of a daughter who is no father
for the god who made her. His is the song
of all fatherless sons, and he sings that suffering
until it becomes an ecstasy, and he lifts
that ecstasy heavenward like a prayer.

A woman searches for God.
She searches kitchens, poems, the wilderness
of heather growing up at her feet.
She watches the sky, looks for the constellation
of sisters, of a vessel opening, spilling water.
She searches yarrow stalks, the broken lines

of trigrams, tarot cards.
She searches her own full breasts,
the wreath of eucalyptus and sweet basil
she hangs above a child's cradle.
The woman has a daughter, and in this child
grows a different dream of divinity:
God in lace, God in a leotard,
God with a girl's face, kneeling beneath a tree.
Beside the black ash tree, fallen, in starlight,
the boy this girl holds plants a garden in her mouth,
and in her throat bloom stars and wounds
and Goethe's *Roslein, Roslein, Roslein.*
What she tastes is the grief of a woman orphaned
for the garden she takes into her mouth,
a woman guilty for a man's solitude,
for a god's grief at his children leaving,
and she sings that lament
until it becomes a possibility,
giedd, giedd, giedd whispering forgiveness,
forgiveness, and a woman's original splendor.

Viaticum

When you love the one you bury, you plan the journey.
My sister and I buried our father with supplies.
His viaticum, his cell phone and a small blue bird,
wings extended in flight, carved from a Polish linden.

In the blue-black tunnel behind my eyes
where the small lightning of sleep sparkles,
there is a linden.

The linden is an ornamental tree and gives birth
to the lime blossom, pungent, nectar-producing, *some say* healing.
Linden wood is soft, easily worked, ideal for crafting
wind instruments, electric guitar bodies, window blinds.

In the blue-black tunnel where the dead lie
and the small lightning of long sleep sparkles,
there is a voice.

My father hummed. He always carried a tune in his head.
My son plays electric guitar, and his voice is old
like Blind Lemon Jefferson or Lightnin' Hopkins.
He carries a shrill breath behind his tongue that rises.

From the blue-black tunnel behind my eyes
birdsong rises and the small lightning of morning
sparkles the living awake.

The day my father died, he used his new cell phone
to call me home. I saved that voice for months until one day
it disappeared among messages set to expire, leaving
in my palm tangled paths of an uncertain ascent.

August Garden

In the August garden in moonlight
the iron bells rust, the wind itself is rust
and silence. What's left of water in the birdbath
becomes the stone which holds it.
The frog, the lilies, all pale green stone.
Green veins on white caladiums
narrow toward stems drooping,
leaning toward the clay.

If I were a child, I would read or kneel,
wait out emptiness till I could feel a rising
in my chest like laughter or blood or song,

but here on the stone steps, I ride
the rhythm of loss. It loosens my hair
at the roots, robs it of color strand by strand.
It pulses blue in the raised veins
in my hands, breasts, in the spreading
veins behind my knees, dirtied blue
marble visible only when I stop,
turn to look back.

A wise man loves water. I long to believe
contentment moves like a river within us,
exceeding time and desire.

August caladiums shine like white stones,
heart-shaped, blank but for vascular
traces of green. I long to believe
these are the traces of rapture
not yet forgotten, bits of green
nourishing the form they inscribe,
sustaining them just above the soil
so that it appears they wait a while,
live as long as they can.

In the Balance of Final Things

Mrs. Schmetterling has been reading *The Egyptian Book*
of the Dead and now when she lies down to sleep
she sees in her mind's eye the balance of final things.
She imagines herself before a tribunal of gods
in human masks. She counts each face like sheep—
old Marx, old Miłosz, one, two. The young Baczyński, three.
Joseph Stalin in a white moustache, baby Adolf in a white smock,
the Black Madonna of Częstochowa, four, five, six.
She sees Europe, east and west, under a sky of fireworks and ash.
She keeps counting, watches the high scales
suspended above her head, one pan drooping
beneath the weight of a single stone.
Mrs. Schmetterling considers her life, waits for the moment
she must place her own heart in the balance.
She wonders what punishment waits for a heart too light.
She regrets laughter, the warmth of her down comforter,
her own fate lucky, random, unearned.

OŚWIĘCIM

I.

I walk through the detritus of history,
a tourist. Our guide is Polish. She knows
each crematorium chimney,
each pond of human ash
will become
a gallery of faces floating
upside down in a smoked glass floor.

We enter the room slowly, almost on tiptoe,
watch whole families recede and rise.
We could fall
into this black glass like water,
rise bleeding, bloated
with tears.

II.

A glass case stretching the full length of a corridor wall
holds sixty years
of braids and strands and mattes
stacked, kilos of a terrible beauty.

Strands of hair move beneath my skin,
a vascular braiding
of heart and lungs and limbs,
blue veins, blue hair
knotted, writhing.
I wake alone,
in a tangle of starched sheets,
unable to cry out or swallow.

III.

The cedars are crowded with ghosts
who wind in and out of the tall trunks,
carrying suitcases,
straightening their caps,
loosening their blouses or vests in the heat.

They are waiting for something.
I can see them.
This is no photograph.

IV.

The streets of Oświęcim are crowded with children.
It is afternoon. School must be out
for they wait at bus stops,
buy ice cream,
crush clods of dried mud with their boot heels.
As far as we can see
the cherries and acacias bloom
white as ice cream, cotton candy,
cumulus clouds rising above a death camp.

BOROWSKI'S SUICIDE

July 1, 1951 six days after the birth of his daughter, Malgorzata

What did he see in that infant face,
ghost of memory, fresh from the belly's gauze,

his palm laid against the tiny skull,
each blue vein in the temple pulsing?

Wrenched from the gauze of memory,
the train car floor littered with children.

Faces flung down, the belly's ghosts.
The floors cleared for the rapes to come,

a young woman, a sheer cotton dress,
the belly's gauze, torn and torn.

Tadeusz Borowski, Polish Catholic,
member of the *Kanada* crew, Auschwitz

survivor, communist, journalist, poet.
A man walking among the living dead

woke one morning to his daughter's face
wrenched from the belly's gauze,

gauze of memory, living ghost swaddled
in the dreamlike pulse of his step.

No stable. No star. No
breath of Elijah at the door.

In Kazimierz

Walking with head bowed,
the shadow of a butterfly on ground ivy,
the soul's movement through this middle earth.

WINTER LITANY

Kraków, March, 2004

I stand on *Wawel Hill*
in early March and morning snow
falls in flocks
tiny paper cranes
descending blowing dissolving
one into another
on the cobblestone walk
an avalanche of light

I believe this must be
what death is

this alternate
shining and melting, shining and flying

How to Paint Light

To paint light you must return to that first raw surface
like the wall of a room

in the lives of rooms you never knew.
Return to sheetrock, shiplap, memoryless stone

or to striations of sun at the bottom of a lake
before shadow accumulates layer by layer.

You must work backwards against pigment,
and dust. Pain and ash. The swift current

of human memory sealing out dawn.
You must close your eyes until you see

your dozing grandmother rock history to sleep.
You are a child in her arms.

What Mrs. Schmetterling Wants

Mrs. Schmetterling wants nothing more
than the landscape, the city's opening
onto streets of stones, shops, small wrought-iron tables
hung with umbrellas, set with cloth napkins, beer.
She meanders among high-rise apartment buildings, window boxes
bursting with petunias, cloud whites, bubble gum pinks,
the purples of bruises, buried blood.
She watches the train station walls blooming with graffiti.
Mrs. Schmetterling does not want history.
She wants the graffiti to color old concrete, cover the blood.
She lives between kitsch and the weight of stones,
the exhibit of painted noses and torsos and giant sunflowers
at the city gate, and the gate itself.
She wants nothing more than her soul's wilderness
taking hold at the city's edge, spreading like milkweed
in the garden plot that no one owns,
no one owns.

Notes

The book's title, epigraph, and that of the title poem, "City that Ripens on the Tree of the World," are taken from Magdalena Tulli's novel *Dreams and Stones* translated from the Polish by Bill Johnston (Archipelago Press, 2004).

"WINDOW"

Stanisław Wyspiański (1869-1907), painter of the Art Nouveau movement in Poland and a colleague of Józef Mehoffer (1869-1946).

"DUSK IN JORDAN PARK"

"Pani" is the formal, respectful second person pronoun "you" in Polish used when speaking to or of a woman.

Jordan Park was established in 1889 by Henryk Jordan (1842-1907) as the first public park and children's playground in Kraków, and the first of its kind in Europe. A Polish physician and professor at the Jagiellonian University, Dr. Jordan was a pioneer of physical education who popularized the idea of public landscapes for physical exercise. This poem refers to the circular labyrinth of hornbeam trees at the park's center where 45 busts of famous Poles, commissioned by Dr. Jordan and created by sculptors Alfred Daun and Michal Korpal, were displayed. During World War II, with the exception of 22 of the busts and a monument of Jordan, the park was entirely destroyed. It has since been re-established and enlarged to 52 acres to include various outdoor sports venues.

"Mrs. Schmetterling Thinks of Her Heart"

Lwów was founded in 1256 C.E. and remained a part of Polish territory through much of the early twentieth century. The city was seized by the Soviets in 1939 and renamed Lvov. From 1941 to 1944 the city was occupied by the Nazis who created the Lvov (or Lemberg) Ghetto, housing about 120,000 Jews nearly all of whom were exterminated. Simon Wiesenthal, famous Nazi hunter and dear friend of Ewa Lipska, was one of the few who survived. In 1945, Lvov became part of the Ukraine under Soviet rule, and was renamed Lviv in 1991 when the Ukraine achieved independence from the USSR.

"The Rothko Chapel, Houston, Early Spring"

"God sent me to the sea for pearls" is a line from one of John Clare's asylum poems written after his psychological collapse in 1837.

"Revisions"

"Roslein, Roslein, Roslein" is a partial line from Goethe's poem "Heidenroslein" ("Rosebud in the Heather") published in 1771. The poem concerns lost virginity and is a dialogue between an urchin boy and a rosebud he finds, plucks from the heather.

"Giedd" in Old English means "song" or "poem," and appears in the final line of "Wulf and Eadwacer" (translated as "Wolf and Wealthwatcher"), an Old English poem in which the female speaker laments her exile and that of the man she loves. The poem implies that she is both responsible for and a victim of this exile which concerns rivalry between the two men of the poem's title. The final line, "uncer giedd geador" ("our song together") implies that the "giedd" they have made is a child. This is one of the few Anglo-Saxon poems spoken by a woman.

"August Garden"

"A wise man loves water" is an aphorism attributed to Confucius.

"Oświęcim"

Oświęcim is the name of the Polish town that became the site of the German death camp Auschwitz-Birkenau.

"In Kazimierz"

Kazimierz is the former Jewish quarter of Kraków, Poland, dating from the 14th century until World War II.

Acknowledgments

I wish to express my gratitude to the editors of the following journals and anthologies in which some of the poems in this volume have appeared:

"The Angel of Architecture," "Revisions," and "Window" appeared in *Tampa Review*.

"The Angel of Architecture" was reprinted in *Improbable Worlds: an Anthology of Texas and Louisiana Poets* edited by Martha Serpas and published by Mutabilis Press. "The Rothko Chapel, Houston, Early Spring" also appeared in *Improbable Worlds*.

"August Garden" appeared in the online journal *qarrtsiluni*.

"In An Amsterdam Hotel" („W jednym z hoteli w Amsterdamie") and "What Mrs. Schmetterling Wants" („Czego pragnie pani Schmetterling") appeared in Polish translation in *Fraza*, a literary journal based in Rzeszów, Poland.

I am grateful to the Houston Arts Alliance for a 2009 New Works Fellowship in Literature awarded through the Individual Artist Grant Program, and to the University of Houston-Downtown for a 2012 Faculty Development Leave Award, for their support in the development of these poems.

My deepest thanks go to Ewa Lipska, Adam Zagajewski, Edward Hirsch, Piotr Florczyk, and to my co-translator, Ewa Elżbieta Nowakowska, for her work on behalf of our translation of Lipska's poetry, for her translation of my own poems into Polish for *Fraza*, for her photograph that appears on the cover of this volume, and for her steadfast friendship across oceans and years. I also wish to thank the members of Calypso Editions collaborative for their careful attention to the crafting of this book.

About the Author

Robin Davidson's poems and translations have appeared in *91st Meridian, AGNI, Literary Imagination, theParis Review, Tampa Review, Words Without Borders,* and the Polish journal, *Fraza.* She is co-translator, with Ewa Elżbieta Nowakowska, of *The New Century: Poems,* from the Polish of Ewa Lipska (Northwestern University Press), and has received, among other awards, a Fulbright professorship at the Jagiellonian University in Kraków, and a National Endowment for the Arts translation fellowship. Her most recent work on Lipska's poetry appears in the fall 2012 issue of *Common Knowledge* (Duke University Press). She teaches creative writing as associate professor of English for the University of Houston-Downtown.

*Calypso Editions is an artist-
run, cooperative press dedicated
to publishing quality literary
books of poetry and fiction with
a global perspective. We believe
that literature is essential to
building an international
community of readers and
writers and that, in a world of
digital saturation, books can
serve as physical artifacts of
beauty and wonder.*

CALYPSO EDITIONS

INFO@CALYPSOEDITIONS.ORG | WWW.CALYPSOEDITIONS.ORG

Pre-order copies of our upcoming titles
CALYPSO EDITIONS
www.CalypsoEditions.org

ATHANOR & OTHER POHEMS

by Gellu Naum; translated by Margento and Martin Woodside

Fall 2013

Almost 15 years after James Brook's translation of Gellu Naum's brilliant prose poem sequence *My Tired Father*, Naum remains almost entirely unknown to English speaking audiences. One of Romania's most important poets and a key figure in the surrealist movement, Gellu Naum stands out as of one of the greatest figures in twentieth-century European poetry—and one of the most sorely under-represented in English language translation. Sampling some of Naum's best work from a unique literary career spanning over more than 60 years, this collection offers a long overdue introduction to some of Gellu Naum's most seminal work.

LITTLE TRILOGY

by Anton Chekhov; translated by Boris Dralyuk

Winter 2013

Anton Chekhov (1860-1904) is universally regarded as a master of the short story, and nowhere is his rich contribution to the genre on fuller display than in the so-called *Little Trilogy* (1898): "The Man in a Case," "Gooseberries," and "About Love." These interconnected stories reflect the entire range of his gifts, his ability to hold comedy in balance with tragedy, to wrest beauty from ugliness, and to transform the pathetic into the sublime. Written rather late in his career, the *Little Trilogy* also serves as a kind of artistic autobiography, charting the evolution of his own approach to story-telling from humorous caricature, to Tolstoyan sentimentality, to a uniquely Chekhovian study of "individual cases," in which generalities are dispensed with and judgment is withheld.

Poetry in translation available from
CALYPSO EDITIONS
www.CalypsoEditions.org

FROTH: POEMS
by Jarosław Mikołajewski
Translated by Piotr Florczyk
ISBN-13: 978-0-9830999-9-4

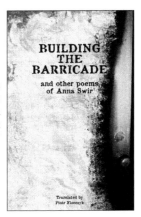

BUILDING THE BARRICADE
AND OTHER POEMS
OF ANNA SWIR
Translated by Piotr Florczyk
ISBN-13: 978-0-9830999-1-8

OF GENTLE WOLVES: AN
ANTHOLOGY OF ROMANIAN POETRY
Translated & Edited
by Martin Woodside
ISBN-13: 978-0-9830999-2-5

Original books available from
CALYPSO EDITIONS
www.CalypsoEditions.org

USE
Poetry
by Derick Burleson
ISBN-13: 978-0-9830999-5-6

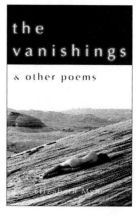

THE VANISHINGS
AND OTHER POEMS
Poetry
by Elizabeth Myhr
ISBN-13: 978-0-9830999-1-8

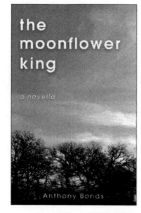

THE MOONFLOWER KING
Fiction
by Anthony Bonds
ISBN-13: 978-0-9830999-4-9

"Calypso Editions looks like a press worth paying attention to."
—Chad W. Post, *Three Percent*